NASSAU

poems and photos by James Duncan

Alpine Ghost Press, First Edition
ISBN: 979-8-218-45565-1
Cover design and all photos by James H Duncan

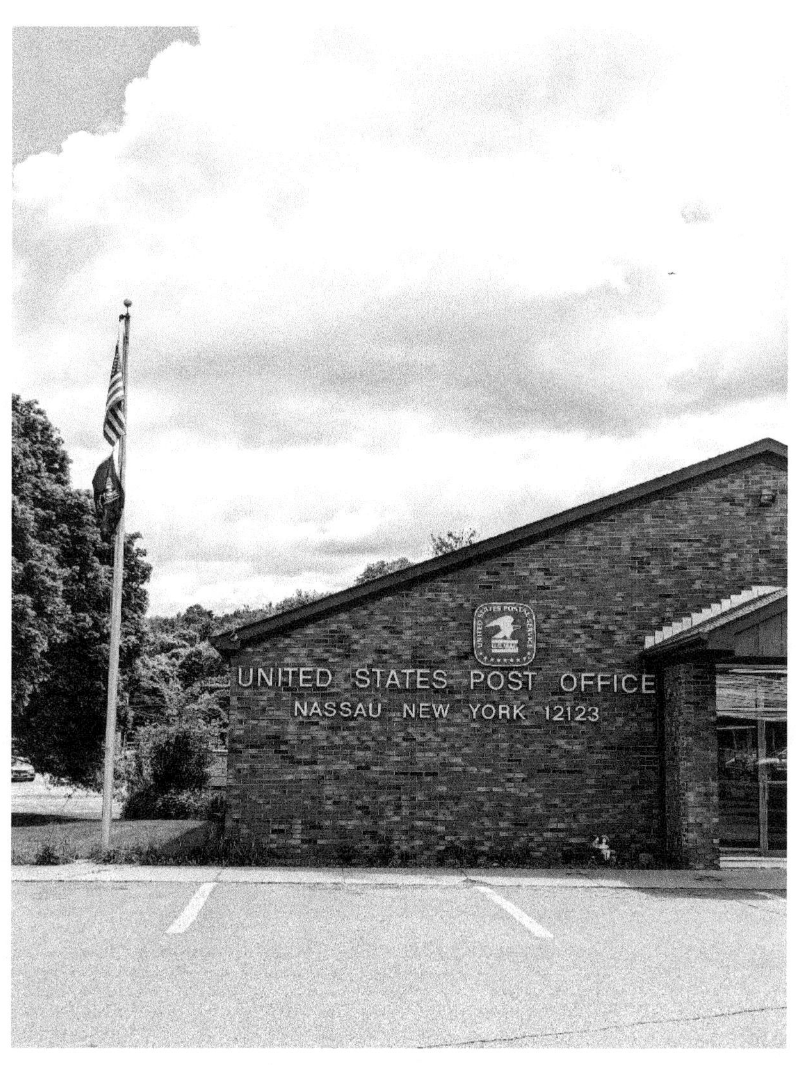
UNITED STATES POST OFFICE
NASSAU NEW YORK 12123

Last night I dreamed that I was a child
Out where the pines grow wild and tall
I was trying to make it home through the forest
Before the darkness falls

- Bruce Springsteen ("My Father's House")

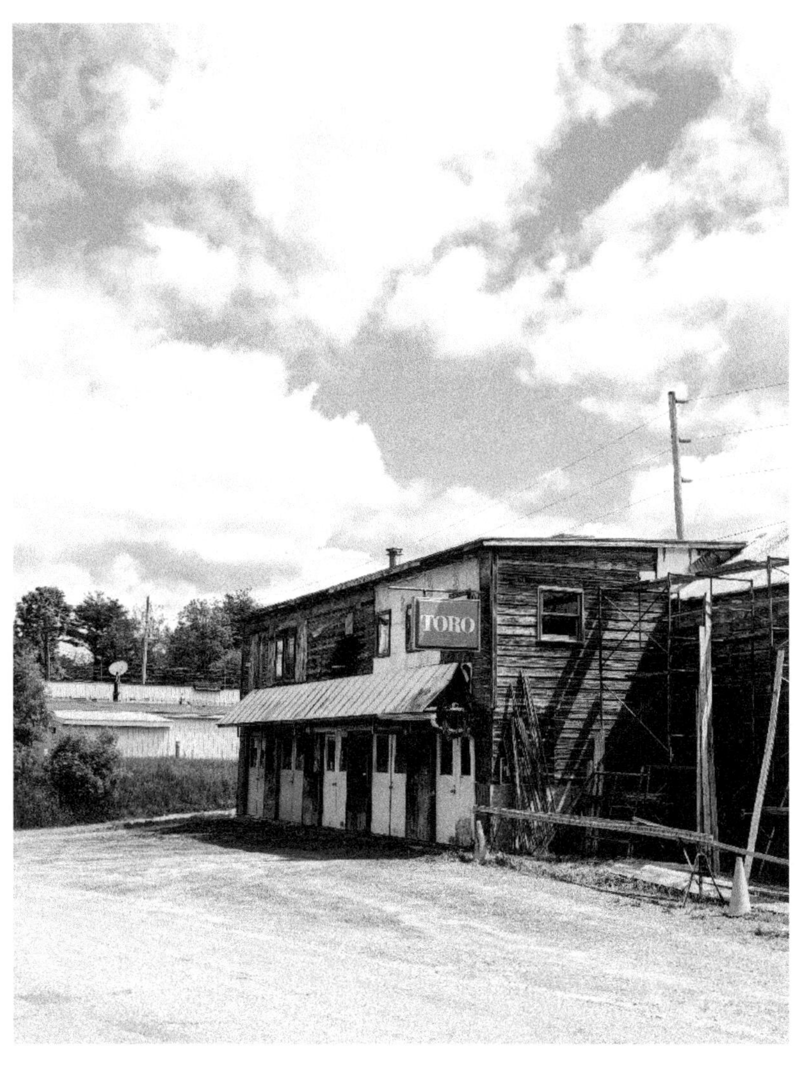
TORO

Nassau

long roads to nowhere
  nestled between fields of
corn and the autumn sun

  my mother and I drove in her
pale yellow station wagon
  back home from the doctors
when the police stopped us
  at a roadblock, asking us if
we'd seen anyone hitchhiking,
  we said we hadn't but that
we'd keep an eye out for anyone

crows filled the power lines like
  informants looking for any
excuse to sing their song as my mom
  and I talked about what it could all
be about as her car weaved through
  hamlets and farms, cornfields and
pine hollows until we reached Nassau

on the news that night we found out
  two teenage girls had killed their
step-mother with a hammer and
  disappeared, the husband coming
home to find his whole family gone

my mother spent the night on the phone
  with anyone who would pick up to talk
about the news while I laid in bed on
  the other end of the trailer listening to her
with the music from *Unsolved Mysteries*
  in the faint background, staring out
my bedroom window at fireflies blinking
  in the yard, wondering if those girls
were out there in the dark, if they'd come
  for me next, if they saw us talking

to the police and county deputies, if all
  the world held secret murderers who
would turn on me in a moment of violence

but in truth the town of Nassau beyond
  the dark forests and cornfields held
only regular folks like us who had to go
  to school and work and grow up to join
unions or armies or lines in supermarkets
  and pay bills that never went away
and mow lawns and feel sad and
  laugh whenever we had the chance as
we got older and older, and almost
  none of them would pick up a hammer
and bludgeon loved ones, almost

all the little towns nearby the very same:
  Castleton, Averill Park, Kinderhook,
too small for something like this, people
  said, *not here, not to people like us*

but it did, and it does, and it will

we heard the news a few days later
  while getting mint chocolate chip
ice cream at Stewarts, that they found
  the two girls, only 14 and 16, that they'd
gone to Burger King after, ate dinner, and
  threw away the evidence in the garbage,
found later by the staff, and they were
  no longer on the run or a threat to sneak
into my trailer window to get me at night

it gave people something to talk about
  as they called their cousins, leaned over
chain-link fences with neighbors, and soon
  enough a war in the desert started and
politicians made speeches and the world
  moved on past Nassau and past our lives

there, and whenever my mom and I passed
  that place where the police set up that
roadblock to ask us about hitchhikers,
  right in front of the house where that one
woman died at the hands of her step-kids,
  I'd think back on that car ride with my
mother, the autumn when I realized
  the world is more complicated than I liked

"that poor man, lost his whole family in
  one night" my mom would say as we passed
and I'd nod and watch the homes fade to
  fields of corn and sunlight and long stretches
of nothingness until we got home, safe and sound

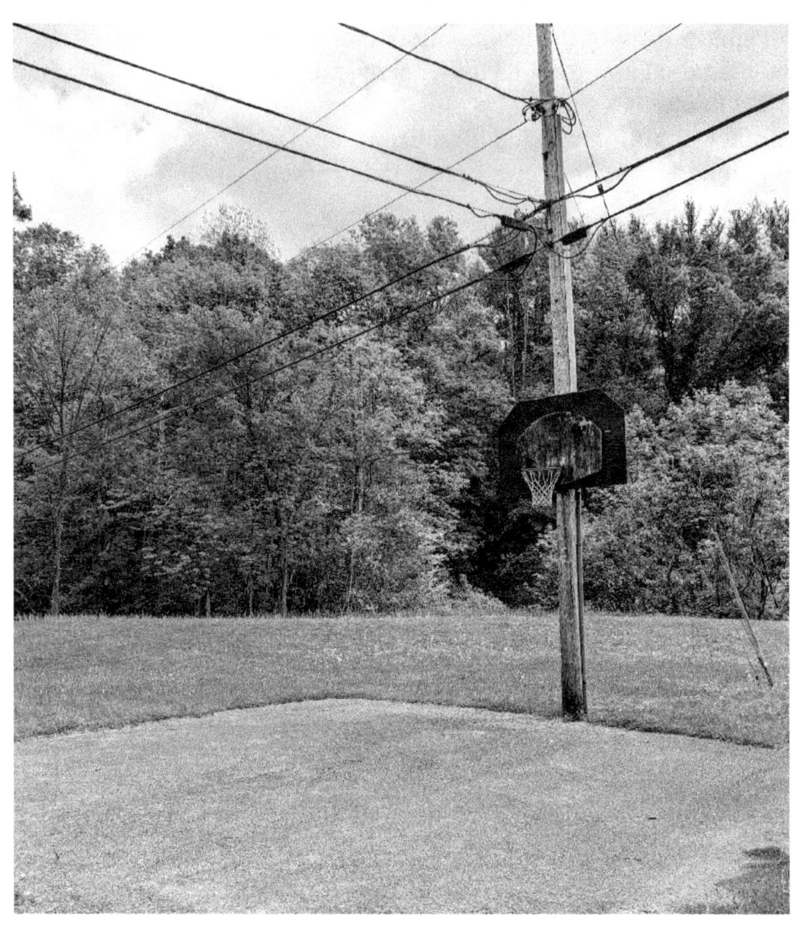

Cedar City

well they paved all the roads leading home
and they tore down the basketball hoop
our old bike jump ravine is overgrown
and our frog pond is just a dried barren reef

the trailer homes all look the same
but the gardens are brighter
the pickup trucks are newer
the faces peering out windows are strangers
living in rooms I wandered as a boy

growing up in a rural trailer park had some perks,
wandering corn fields and cedar swamps,
pine forests in the wintertime, racing
streams in the summertime, all the time
in the world to explore the topography of our youth
until we found out quick that the clock stopped
ticking and we kept going, going, gone

now here we are, strangers
on the gravel streets we used to rule,
streets now paved, streets cracked with age,
streets washed away in inevitable
nuclear fallout or cataclysmic chicanery,
leaving behind the many ghosts of the future
who sometimes come back to the here and now

but the dead aren't dead yet,
though coming back hasn't made me
more alive, just a little less solvent, as if
I bury a part of myself under the old
basketball hoop every time I return to
wander Cedar City Trailer Court, observe
what was and what never will be again

The Furnace of Your Heart

she sleeps through anything, any fight, any
cold weather snap, her blonde hair
splayed silver in the moonlight coming down
through busted venetian blinds

and all you can do is think about what she said,
how it don't matter that you ain't goin'
anywhere, that no one is goin' anywhere anyhow,
but neither of you have seen thirty yet
and you just can't understand how that kind of
thinking can linger in the bones so early

it's cold and you can't afford to turn up the heat,
can't afford new thermal underwear,
she snores, a soft whistle through her nose that
you only hear when the apartment is so
silent it almost hurts to open your eyes and see
what has become of the two of you

no one hears you close the door, boots crunch the
thin rind of hoarfrost on the sidewalk
down the street past the ballfield, past Stewart's
and the hardware store, through the
center of town to the Village Pizza II and the door in
back where Ricky's is still open after hours,
the uneven bar and dozen rickety stools, a tavern so narrow
you need to walk down the bar sideways,
and it ain't Ricky at the bar (he's been dead five years)
but Hank Jesper, who knows what you want
and you sip your PBR in silence with two other midnight
drinkers, no music, no conversation, no warmth
save for the hopes you held on to for maybe too long
now tossed into the furnace of your heart,
burning and simmering to light the way into a future you
never wanted, but a future you now realize you
could never avoid, just like everyone else in this damn town

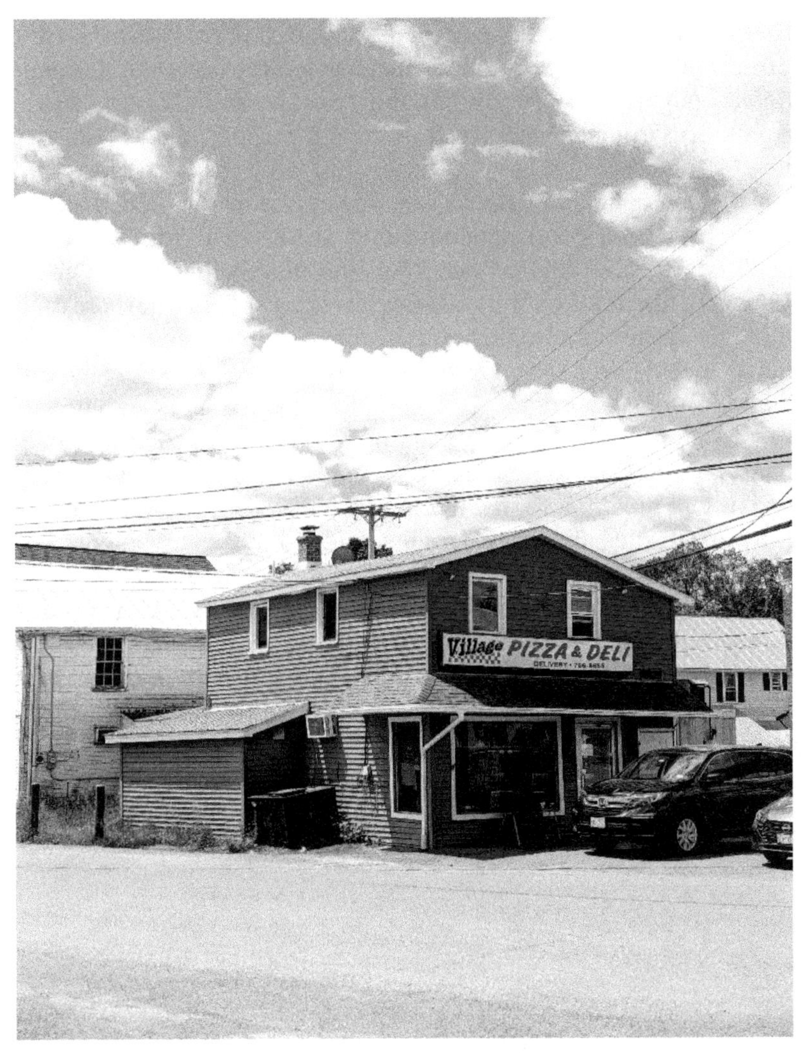
Village PIZZA & DELI

Carousel of Will and Might

summer storms impend and whisper through the trees lining Elm Street and carry the cool flagellates beyond the town line through nooks and neighborhoods hugging the shore of Nassau Lake, rippling its ruined waters and sweeping through the forests out into Van Gogh fields of rolling gold and roadside dust, the cornfields young and stunted, the old summer camp cabins on the shore of Smith Pond abandoned to secrets and rotting in the ageless sun, now blotted out by roiling thunderheads, the cows lowing in the fields over by Krouner Road, and then—just cresting the hills as the first droplets of rain come with tentative clatter—a horse appears, free from constraint and all alone, no saddle, no bit, walking along the ridge overlooking farms and trailers and the dirt road leading back to town, breaking into a sprint as the rain falls harder, no destination, no escape, exploding in a carousel of will and might, breaking for the treeline, disappearing into the pines as the rain steadies and blots out all sound, all other movement save for clouds moving ever eastward and the occasional toll of thunder, mother nature seeking out its lost titan as the gray skies turn purple, then black, and then the rains disappear altogether, leaving nothing but the lights of town on the distant horizon

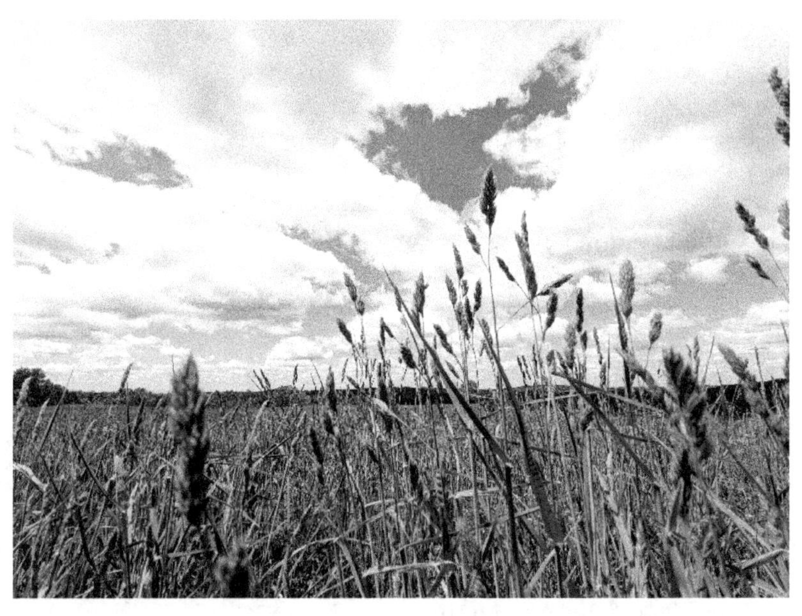

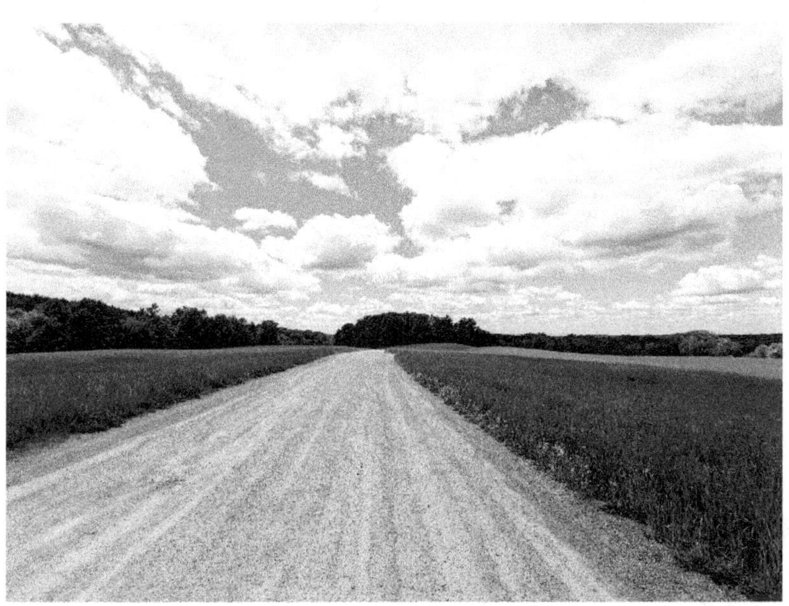

Hand-Me-Downs

here among the hand-me-downs
the Tupperware and cats
the scratched and clawed coffee
table, brown couch, local news

the baby gnawing melba toast
the sunlight cutting shapes
I have a kingdom of stains
and silence so loud I could cry

here is here, and you are there
a car and a highway, a shirt I
iron and sew, a lunch I pack,
a place to be, far from Nassau

a desk and a clock, a break room out there,
full of gossip and secretaries,
Jack and Paul from Accounting,
the score from a game I don't understand

I asked you not to make me keep it
but you said God watched
us both from above, judged me,
and so I built its bones inside my body

and now the baby crawls across
the stained carpet, soggy melba toast
ground into the fibers, and I wait for
your 'there' to become 'here' at dusk

but sun set hours ago and there remains
there, while here there are cries of
hunger, cries of wonder, cries
that cannot answer the questions that remain

why does no one tell you the end will
come so early in towns like this?

why does the sun set just that once
and never rise again, no matter the shapes

crawling gold across my body
the morning they found us,
melba toast ground into the fibers
here among the hand-me-downs?

County Route 7

it whispers across County Route 7,
the filthy wind lapping filthy water,
  rancid and spoiled for a minor wealth
no one in this town will ever see

none of us knew why the waters
of Nassau Lake palpitate toxic waste,
  a chemical spill, town dump run-off,
none of us knew what happened

some say it's the mining and the quarry
on the far eastern side of the town line
  a local family with its name on everything
in sight and half of it out of sight too, but

we only sensed something had tainted
this land, this water, the silt around
  the edge of the lake no good, the little
fish fry shack on its shore no good

always drove by, never stopped,
painted red, white, blue, thick stripes
  with a fish on the sign, a rusted Pepsi
display hanging from the awning

some of us in the trailer park once talked
about collecting our quarters and dimes
  to walk along County Route 7 for a snack
at the shack, two hours round-trip on foot

but Candy and Becca laughed it off with
talk about all of us growing third eyes or
  other strange appendages young boys
wouldn't want, all because of bad fish

straight from the lake—they said, catch 'em,
fry 'em, sell 'em to rubes like you for a buck

but go if you want, what do we care if you
mutate into roadkill along County Route 7

so we never went, but one imagines if we did, the
horrors we'd become, some Innsmouth creature
with gills of our own, who knows? only the filthy
wind lapping the filthy waters of Nassau Lake

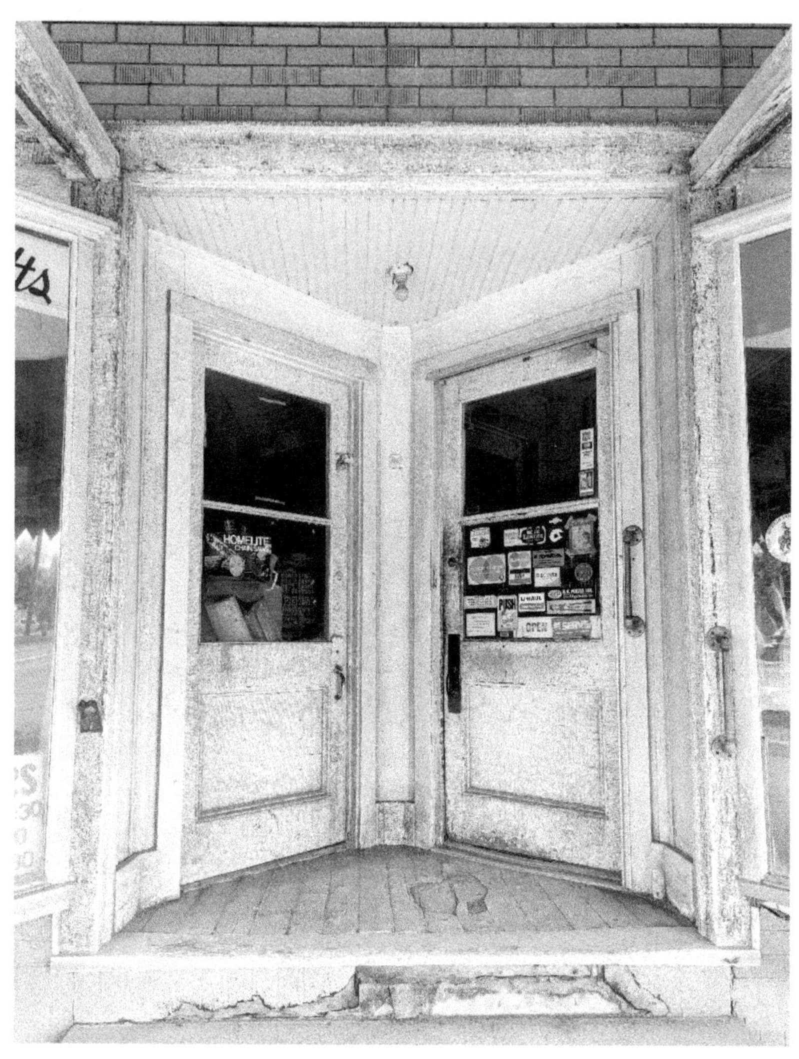
HOMELITE
PUSH
OPEN

Village Video

choices made and fumbled on Saturday nights
in Action, in New Release, in the little booth in
the rear where men go alone, an open secret, and
take home plastic love in shame, but over in Horror
the thick tape cases have the best covers and we'd
congregate in awe at the gruesome promises in
each one, finally picking a slasher, the one about
the kids at summer camp who get what's coming
to them, plus a game for after: Zelda or Gauntlet,
pay the man at the counter and push through the
heavy double doors into the sultry summer night
to walk the sidewalks of Nassau home, holding on
to what innocence we have before the neon lights
of Village Video go dark for good and we're left to
face the horrors of the world with no sword, magic,
or Hollywood finale to save us from what lies in wait

Johnny '89

maybe he'll like baseball
they're painted on the wall
bats and gloves and blue skies
in newborn anticipation

but all he does is cry his eyes raw
and all I can do is whisper while
the front door slaps shut, dad on his
way for cigarettes / to clear his head

as down the hall mom sits facing
the wall, the radio playing Elton John
singing about the blues, then weather,
traffic on the hour, static on the mind

I know dad isn't coming back tonight
heard it in the way the door slapped shut
"Mikey, keep an eye on the house" he once
called out, off to Ricky's or some other bar

I always do: watch and pray and wonder
what comes next, another song on the radio,
another ragged howl from Johnny in the crib,
another cigarette run that might never end

but the door opens again and I hear his boots
come down the hall and he smells of Camels
and sweat, picks up the baby and sways in place
while the radio down the hall plays softly, softly

I stand beside him as streetlights turn on outside
and Johnny stops crying: "there ya go…there ya go"
his boots headed back down the hall as I stand still in
the dark, fearful any move will ruin what light remains

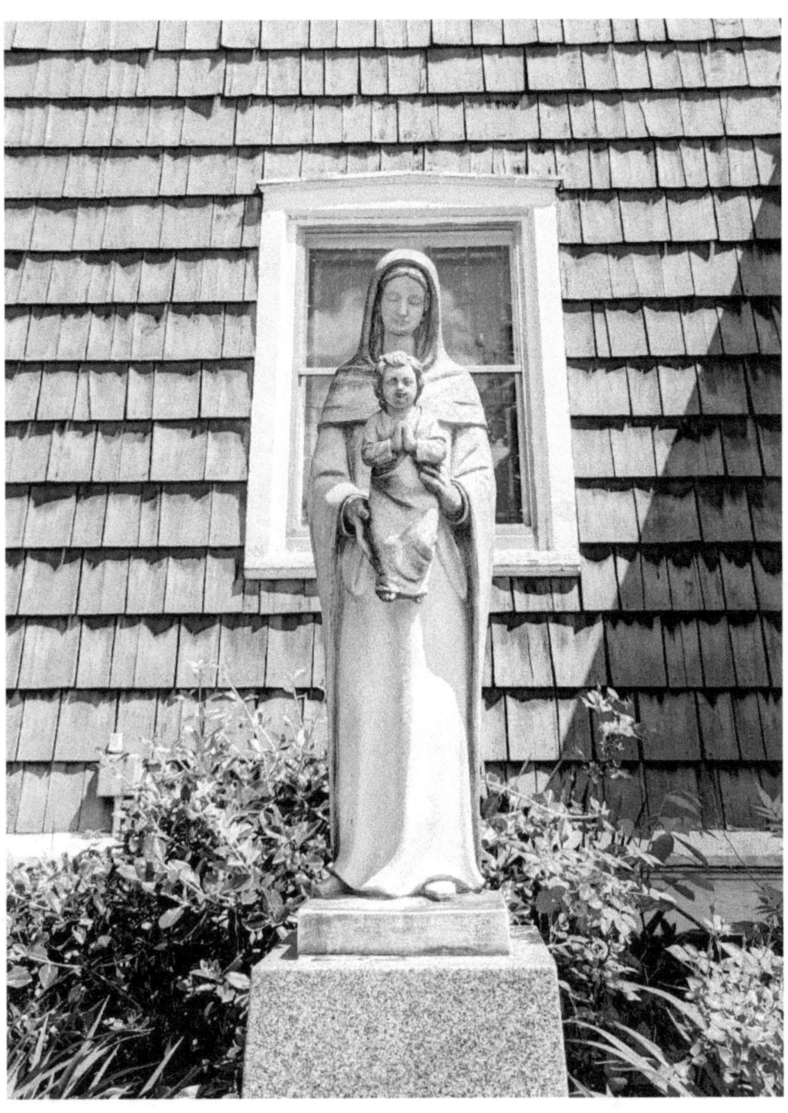

Free Library

petite
lilies of
the valley
dapple
the green
patchwork
of grass in
front of
the small
free library
with white
shutters
and a flag
wavering
on the edge
of town
where one
page of
my heart
resides
in silence
waiting
on a world
that keeps
passing by
in search
of anything
else to see

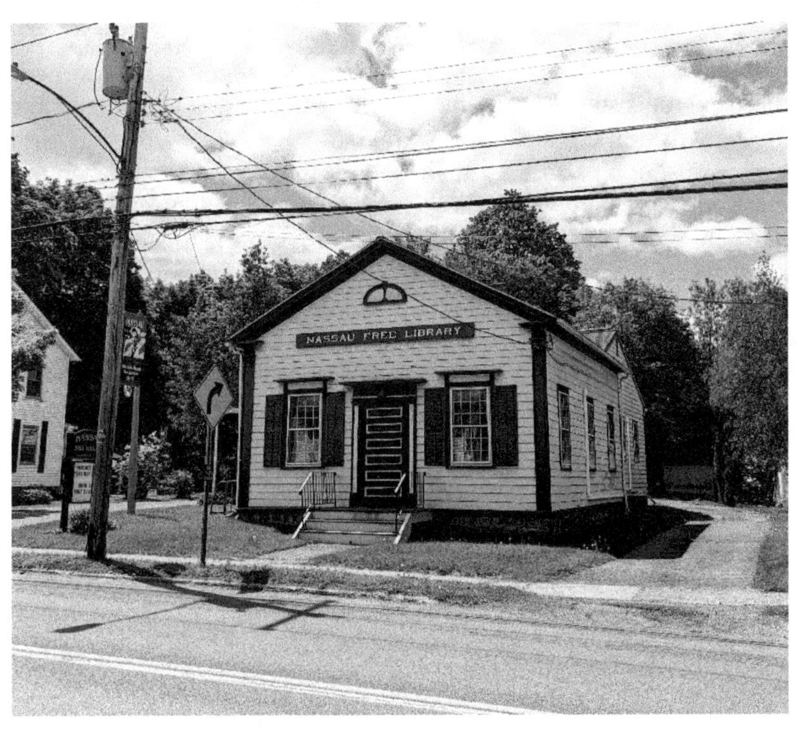
NASSAU FREE LIBRARY

Cherry Dip

sat on a bench outside of Smiley's Ice Cream on Main Street just in time to see a state trooper pull over a lanky scarecrow of a young man with a mange-riddled face, the cruiser's reds and blues reflecting all throughout the village downtown // by the time the cherry dip on my cone cracked into shards, the man was in handcuffs crying on the curb and the trooper began rifling through the trunk and stacking the bags of drugs on the roof, looking for all the world like pouches of baking soda \\ as eight-year-old girls on bikes ride past ringing their bells // the sun sets deep into the west where Albany might be if you closed your eyes and thought hard enough, but horizons are hard to imagine with steel on your wrists with a whole ice cream shop watching your future dissolve into a melted pool of vanilla twist on the asphalt \\ an hour later it never happened, never existed // children continue to bike home and teenagers go on asking for rainbow sprinkles on their sundaes, futures clear and bright in the lights of Smiley's Ice Cream down on Main Street

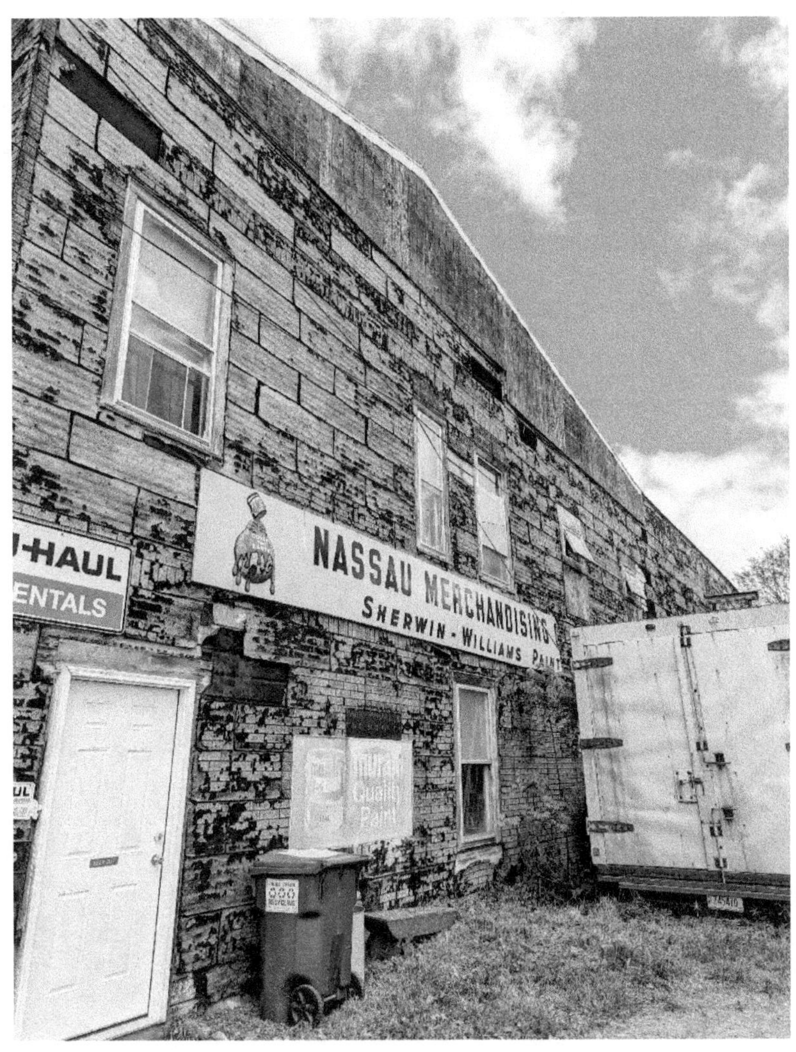
-HAUL
ENTALS
NASSAU MERCHANDISING
SHERWIN - WILLIAMS PAINT
Quality
Paint

Grand Hotel

never was a hotel from what I could see,
maybe the kind you'd find in old westerns,
a mere house in a desolate town, and in a way
that's what it is here too, a town fading by
the year with no need for a hotel, grand or
otherwise, but the signage remains, the hope
and possibility, hollow as it may seem in
the rusty sunset tumbling through town tonight

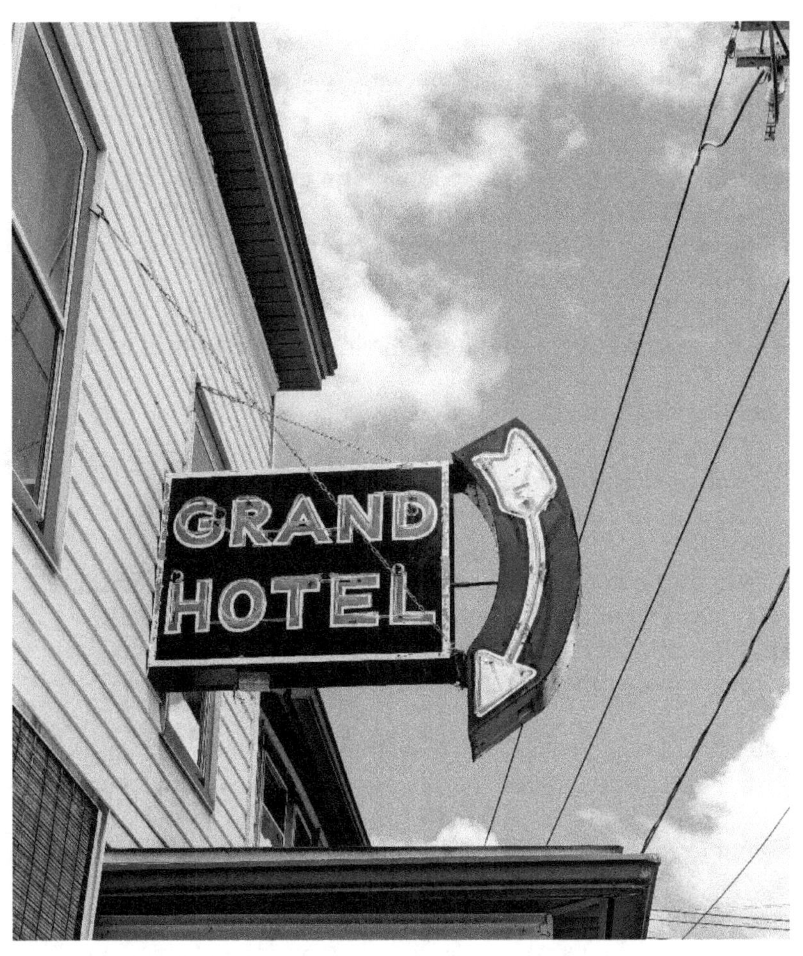
GRAND
HOTEL

Greener Meadows

instead of DPS Elementary right in Nassau, they
    bussed us out past the interstate to Green Meadow
for K through 4, but I put in an extra year because
    they said I was too emotional for a kindergartener

they said I wet myself one too many times and that
    I cried too much, that I didn't like sports and I sat
alone at lunch after my girl friend (not girlfriend,
    too young for all that) asked me to open
her Star Crunch wrapper but I used my teeth and
    she cried so I got time-out alone in an empty room

long tiled halls of canary yellow and beige, bathrooms
    green and brown, everything leftover from the 1960s,
the radiators, the window crank-handles, the plumbing,
    little library chairs scuffed from generations of shoes

I spent as much time in the library as I could, rainy afternoons
    in October and May, lights dim in the back where they
kept the older books, the dictionaries and the memoirs,
    the books of the occult and ghosts, which I liked best

even then I wasn't sure how they allowed us to read them,
    books of werewolves and poltergeists, books of witchcraft,
tales of alien abductions and fortune telling and possessions,
    but I read them all, one by one in the shady back corner alone

and reading those books, it made my drives home on the bus
    much more interesting, passing graveyards and abandoned
churches and warehouses, places where ghosts might wander,
    and I wondered then about my trailer on the outskirt of town

would I abandon its rooms one day too? graduate and leave
    for greener meadows, spiders and shadows growing wild in
my little closet, in the hall, in our open-concept living spaces
    would my spirit peer out from old dirty windows and spy on
those who wandered by as the weeds overtook our trailer walls?

perhaps, I thought as I closed another book of ghost tales and
    turned out the light, going to sleep for another day of gym
and missed homework and daydreaming about what else
    this world of ghosts, ghouls, and detention might hold

Deafening Silence of Midnight's Reply

How many abandoned gas stations can one town have?
How many times can you recycle an empty storefront?
Didn't there used to be a pharmacy, a dentist, a cafe here?
Didn't we once feel the astronomical tide in this place?
What happened to all the elms that once lined Elm Street?
What happened to that shop that sold comics and candy?
Was there really a topless bar behind NAPA autoparts?
Was Nassau once a field of dandelions and glacial silence?
Why did sadness stain every weekday night in this town?
Why do these memories flicker and fade like fireflies?

don't regret or think too hard in the silence of the night,
there are few hours left, and dawn comes sooner than you think

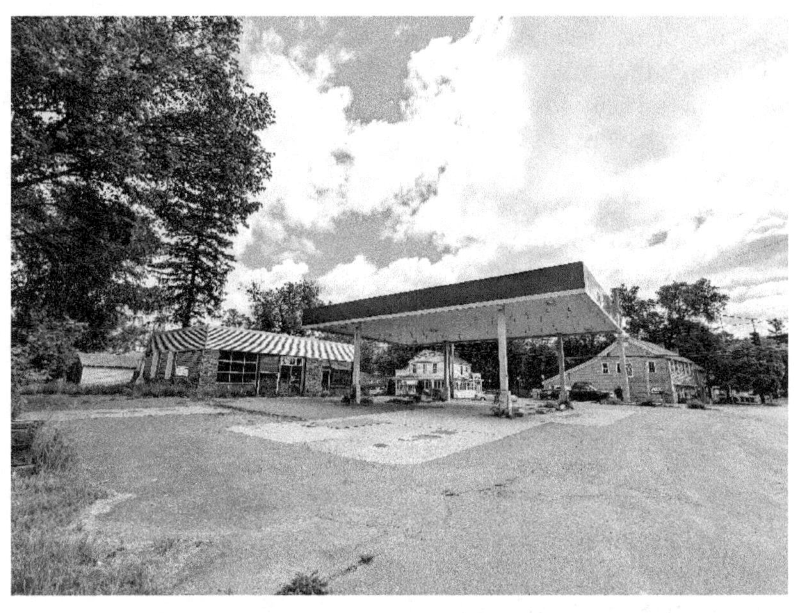

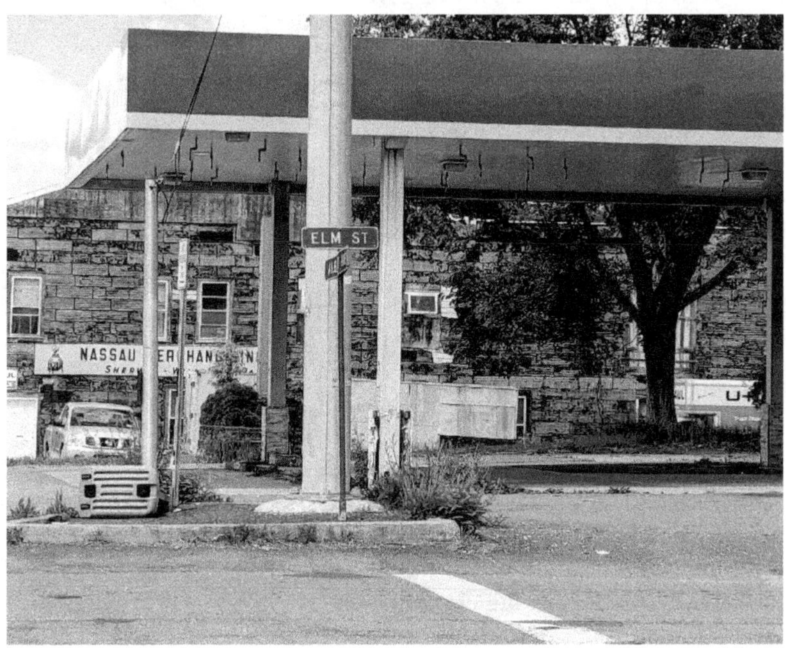
ELM ST
NASSAU

Funny Cars

you could hear the cars
all through the valley
and sometimes all the way
to the edge of Nassau

drag racers, funny cars,
the dirt buggies spinning
out in the racing pit as the
crowds cheered in the stands

the smell of gasoline and
burned oil omnipresent on
the wind, and after fireworks
at night: gray ghosts overhead

you go with Bobby and Guy and
Guy's new step-dad, each of you
get a $5 grab bag he offers to win
over your approval, which you give

a cheap t-shirt with a monster truck
print, a sticker, a plastic coin purse
that says Lebanon Valley Speedway
on its glossy yellow rubber siding

you don't know a damn thing about
cars or racing but you agree to go 'cause
your mom wants you out of the house on
her Saturday off from cleaning homes

you'd rather have walked to the free
library on Main Street than this, but
Guy's step-dad buys you all Cokes too
so you can stand the ear-splitting roar

the funny cars don't seem so funny, they
just make you deaf to the cheers of Guy

and Bobby, and you come to realize just
because you're neighbors, you ain't friends

Bobby takes your sticker and gives you
his coin purse, saying they're for sissies
and laughs with Guy 'til you shove him
off the fifth bleacher up, straight down

pops his tooth out, bleeds on his new tee,
and screams at you the whole ways home,
Guy's new step-dad is angry for missing the
last six drag races, but that's too bad

just as you climb into his '85 LaSabre
you see your assistant principal dressed
in racing gear, helmet under his arm, and
he waves, asked if you're doing okay

and you wonder what to say to Mr. Smith,
if you're ever gonna to be doing okay, if you
should lie and beg him to take you home,
or let you sit co-pilot in his drag race car

but you nod and say you're fine, good luck,
and he gives you a smile as he walks away
and you never speak to Mr. Smith again, but
you don't know that yet on the long drive home

Townie Cops

a state trooper up by the highway exit
once pulled us over and said, "Nassau,
huh? I wouldn't trust a Nassau townie
cop as a paperweight. Don't let them
catch you doing half a mile over 20 in
that town, ya hear?" and let us off with
a warning, pulling around and turning west
back toward the big city lights of Albany
twinkling behind us as we continued on
to the darkened hollows and trailer parks,
the huddled forests and empty gas stations,
the village streets and run-down homes
where we came from, a town even the
law cannot abide without shaking their
weary heads in baffled shame and derision

Blade and Salt

plow blade grattles and rakes the snow into embankments
all through the village, ten inches and falling all day

my old man rides shotgun, thermos of coffee and Baileys
steaming from his lap, AM talk radio and idle chatter

it's his old truck, the town plow they won't or can't replace;
he points where he once hit a car, once took out a mailbox

falls back into silence, sipping coffee, eleven inches and falling;
I make another pass through Lake Shore Circle Drive, homes

huddled against the wind and ice coming off Nassau Lake,
no one on the road except the two of us, the blade and the salt,

tree branches reaching over the road like the antlers of an elk
frosted white and groaning under the weight of winter and age

my old man, out of nowhere, says he misses his brother, says
he didn't mean to let their relationship die before he died too

says it'll snow past midnight and falls into silence as we pass
the old fish fry shack on Route 7 on the way back into town

we wait at the red light on Elm Street, my old man snoring
softly, and I think I don't want this to end, the storm, this life

just let the snow keep coming, the years, the idle chatter;
twelve inches and falling as the plow blade grattles and rakes

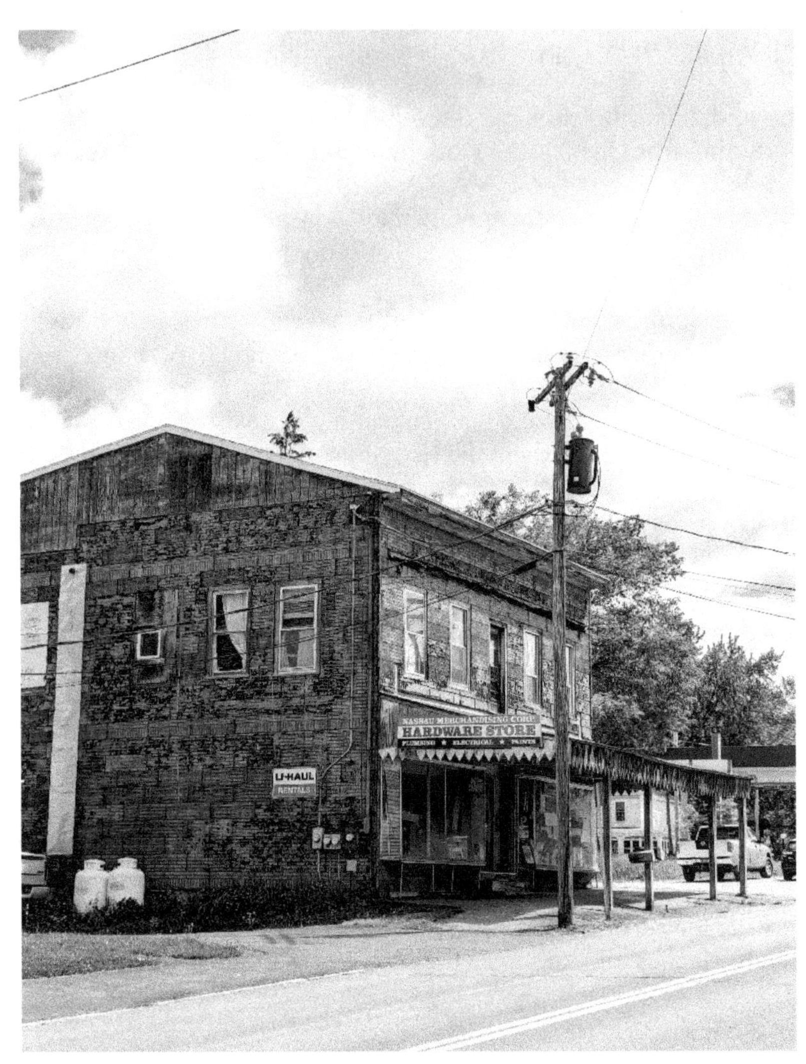
NASSAU MERCHANDISING CORP.
HARDWARE STORE
PLUMBING ★ ELECTRICAL ★ PAINTS
U-HAUL
RENTALS

Bailey's Hardware

born ancient into this world
a two-story hardware store tilted
and faded with chipped paint like so
many autumn leaves falling red
yellow and brown from signs for
motor oil, chainsaws, Stanley, DeWalt,
Toro, barrels full of rakes out front,
Saturday afternoon collapsing into
sunset glinting off the 20 MPH sign, half
hidden to trap out-of-towners, tickets by
the dozen, and even locals couldn't stand
the townie Nassau cops who'd park
out of sight between Bailey's Hardware
and the Sunoco station, a single island
with one pump for diesel, one for unleaded,
$1.59 a gallon sign overhead, askew and
rusted, born ancient into this world
and not getting any younger as Saturday
night succumbs to Sunday, one red light
flashing silent in the center of Nassau town,
an intersection to nowhere, no way out,
just red lights reflected all night in the
windows of Bailey's Hardware store, nuts &
bolts, work gloves half-off, waiting just for you
to come and bring them anywhere else
and give them purpose, give them life

Sunday Supplication

Sunday at Saint Mary's and the pews are half full
and those who came kneel on red velvet stools
and whisper to themselves, the priest's head at
the alter lowered in silence; I watch the light filter
down through stained glass depictions of Mary
and Peter and shepherds carrying lambs in their
arms, eyes rolled back in supplication to some
power above, as down here the prayers end and
everyone shakes hands as the organ bleats another
hymn and we go on with our lives as if anything
changed from the Sunday before when the light
showered down through rolled eyes and lambs
wool made of glass, a gift from above that keeps
on giving, and keeps us right where He wants us

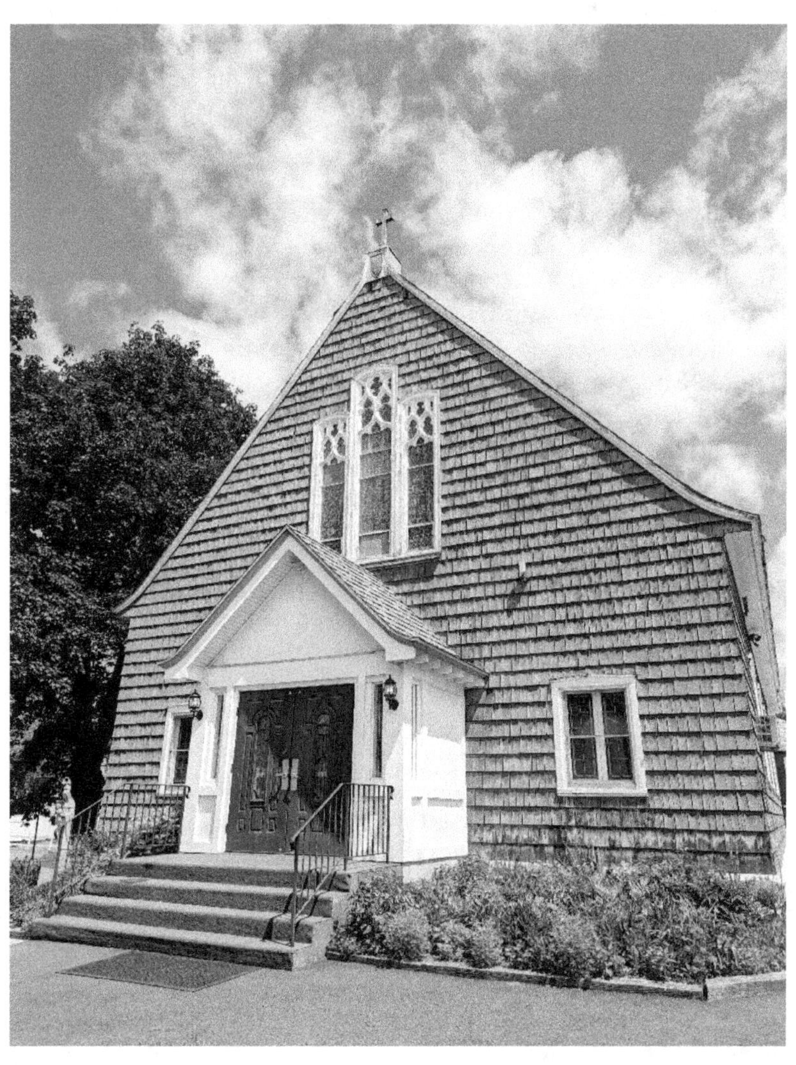

The End of the Route

Our bus stop is a little worn patch of grass where the trailer park entrance met Krouner Road. A corn field across the way stretched to the far treeline, often shrouded with mist in the morning. When the bus arrived, I'd climb on hoping for a window seat, allowing for some escape, some time to be alone. I'd settle in to stare across at the fading mist that snaked through the emerald cornstalks and the pine boughs far beyond, put on my headphones, listen to my U2 cassette my father mailed me. Countryside views rolled by bucolic, and we'd slow at this remote farmhouse or that lonely trailer. We always waited longer for this catholic school kid we picked up and dropped off at Holy Spirit before going to our own school. She ran out in her house on the hill, her plaid skirt billowing, backpack swinging on her back, hair in the wind, a stoic kid who always sat up front. It was the only time I ever saw her in my whole life, running to or away from that bus. Never again, never since. I sometimes listen to "With or Without You" now and think of her, wonder if that little girl is still there waiting for Bus #24 to drive up. Later we'd pass the cluster of houses along Nassau Lake. With so many homes so close together right on the water's edge like that, with so many kids waiting to get on the bus, it felt as if it should have been its own town, something different from Nassau proper, and that they should have a shop where kids could buy soda and comics and candy in the summer, and their parents could buy beer and smokes and cereal, etc. They'd all play by the lake and the town would be called Blue Sky maybe, the clouds and sun reflecting right off the water. Only later did I learn that Nassau Lake was contaminated, gutted of fish, devoid of drinkable water, a grimy place, all because some rich family who owned a mining company let their waste seep into the earth. No wonder no shop opened up. No wonder the area hadn't grown. No wonder my daydreams were just that. It was only a tiny crossroads in the middle of tainted Americana. Our route to school passed through Nassau proper and a few different small hamlets before we got to East Greenbush, which always felt like such a big town when I was little. Each village along the way had its own curious-looking shops and storefronts that made me think, "These places are special. These places are where we go when we need things and they'll always be there." In truth, they were sad little shops, small and hardly used, dilapidated, eking out an existence, like the greasy-spoon diner standing between the second-rate car dealerships along County Routes 9 & 20. Some changed over time, like the Hess station that became the Exxon that became the Speedway. Some hadn't changed in years, like Miller's Auto shop, a tiny thing that always looked half-abandoned but like someone might show up and dust off the windows and keep working on cars. But they never did. I wondered which one I'd become, an evolutional blossom who found a way through to something worthwhile, or something burdened by the weight of my past, dusty and scarred, closed to the world and living in shadow. I always hope for the former, and always feared the latter, a grim existence that waited for each of us at the end of the route.

My Mother's House

a bedroom for each of us,
washer and dryer, dishwasher, porch
yard of dirt and clay, tap water she'd later
discover was spoiled, but it was new
and it was hers
her first home
her first deep breath
free
from husbands and fathers
with blue shag carpet, 72 feet long
more than a trailer home
a home
a home
two children and a home
a yellow station wagon that might still run,
and looking back I can't imagine
how scared she was, how nervous,
how eager, and of course how
brave

Used Cars

A '91 Pontiac with rust stains on the roof. We took it up and down the streets in town, passed the ball fields and the gun shop and took a right at the Sunoco station back to the edge of the village. On the first turn I could tell the CV joints were going out but all she did was stare out the passenger window and tell me how she didn't like this town. She had to get out. It was going to trap her like it did her sister. The faint smell of smoke came from the air vent. I wasn't sure if it was residual ghosts of old cigarettes or maybe the engine. The gauge said the temp was fine but that didn't mean anything. She put her feet on the dash. Bare and pale in the early summer sun. I thought of footprints, but who cares? I wasn't buying this old Pontiac anyway. Not from Jeff at the Fix-n'-Go outside of town. Not after he made that racist joke about what PONTIAC (as an acronym) stands for. I'd heard it a million times. I mean, on one hand, who cares. But I'd heard too many guys I went to school with (who reminded me of Jeff at the Fix-n'-Go) who belittled my best friend, a half-Mexican, as a "spic" or "wetback" and I made the decision at age nine not to fully trust anyone who said such dumb shit. Another turn. Another cul-de-sac. The wind played with her hair. Caramel whippets dancing around the headrest. She sometimes joked about robbing a bank and she smelled like a department store perfume counter, and I like both of those things. She sighed, looked at me. I winked. Maybe it was too late for us to get out. I pulled into the Fix-n'-Go garage beside the line of used cars and told Jeff I'd like to try the '88 LeSabre too. He said he had to find the key. I said that was fine, I didn't have anywhere to be. I'll bet when he came back out to find us gone, he was pissed. But to hell with Jeff Sawyer. We headed to Smith Pond. Watching the way her feet bobbed above the water and caught the light of the sun as she tried to float with the abandoned summer camp on the hill was worth another week of hunting used cars, just something to get us from Point A to anywhere but here.

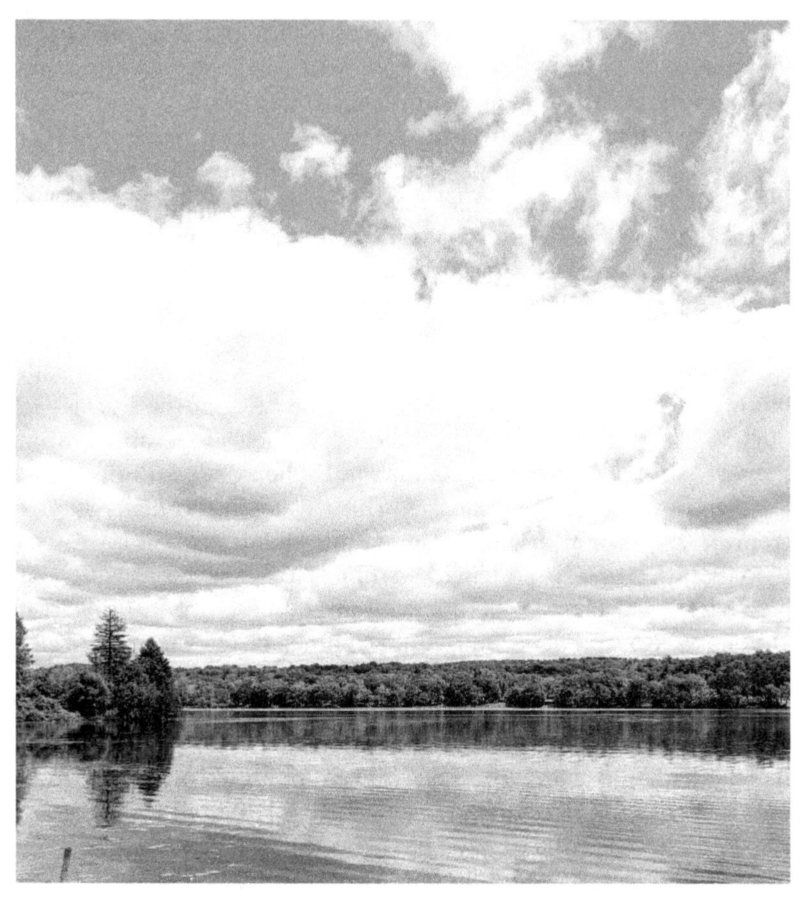

Lyons Lake

I find scattered kindling and stoke a
fire in the small cement pit, then I sit
as the smoke coils into the morning fog,
all the pine trees and the tall grass and
the water of the lake looking grayscale in
all that smoke rising and spreading out
to all reaches of the world, while here
on the edge of Lyons Lake on the coldest
summer morning I can recall, I can hear
the camp counselors down at the resort
get ready for their day, dragging the
canoes to the edge of the water for
the summer camp kids to use, a ball
bouncing somewhere in the faint
distance, kickball maybe, I don't
know what they do, the endless
mornings of the youthful, while
here life winnows down to coals
as if someone has forgotten to
stoke the fire, add the wood,
tend the flames to light the
way to something better
than a dilapidated shack
on the edge of a lake no
one will remember if
enough summers
pass us by into
the smoke and
fog, to graves
waiting just
for you
and
me

Bone Garden

just south of town on Route 203
there's a bone garden of clustered green
maples and slate gray headstones
where Uncle Lyle sleeps with his memories
of watching Red Sox games all summer long,
where Aunt Bea sleeps with her potato salad
recipe, the one with the pickles and mustard,
where Uncle Ray hides his silent sadness
about what Agent Orange did to his life,
where Grandpa Jackson continues to ignore
his wife, his kids, his siblings in eternal slumber,
hiding that one dark secret he kept for so long,
it's a place where every old man playing horseshoes
at the family BBQs of my youth now lies,
where every whispering aunt at Sunday mass
now prays with bowed heads, hands crossed,
surrounded by silk and earth and silence,
a place where the wind blows lonely in March
and the sunlight glows orange neon in October,
we pass by there a hundred times a year,
heading down to Chatham or Kinderhook or home again,
and each time we offer up a passing glance,
a flickering memory, an unspoken acknowledgement
that soon enough we too will lie down among the
grassy knolls and slate gray stones to tend our own garden
of memories that will one day fade to nothing but wind

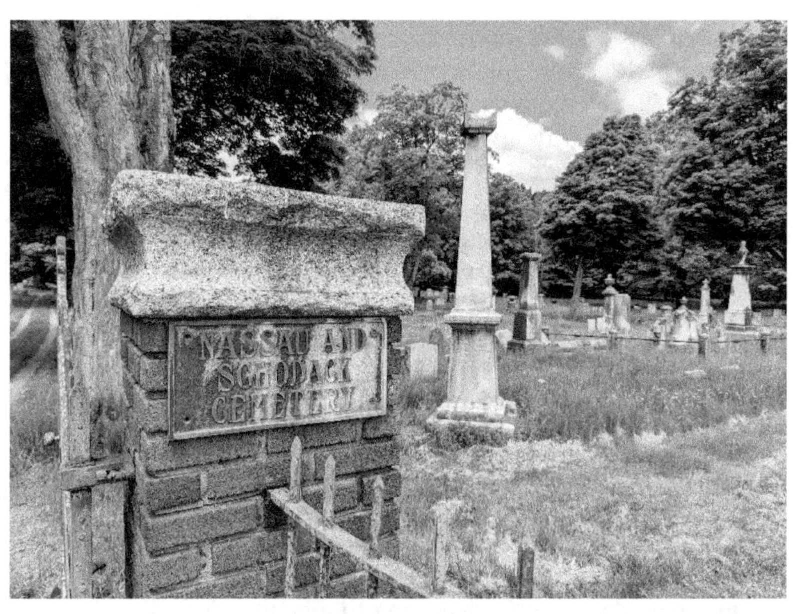
NASSAU AND
SCHODACK
CEMETERY

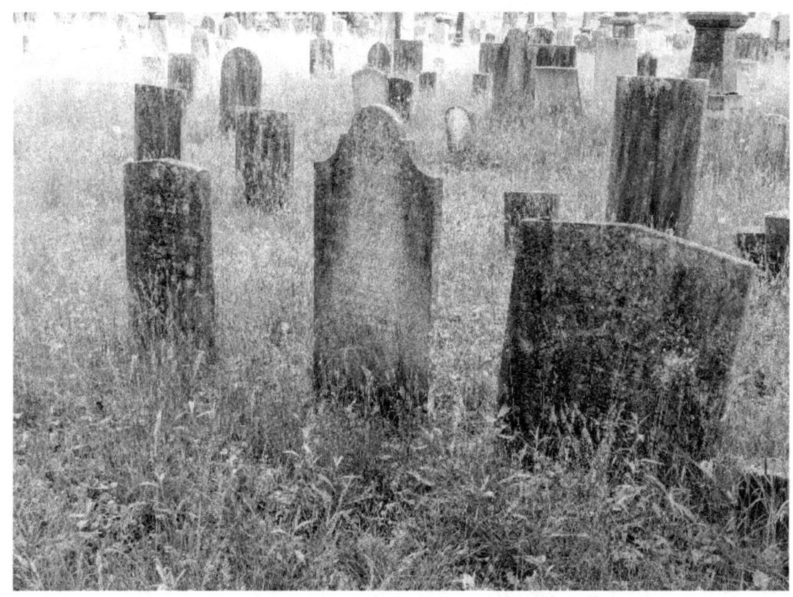

Jane of John Street

grew up in a Victorian on Elm, settled
into a saltbox on John, just up the street
from DPS, the elementary school where
all their kids went—convenient, cute, calling
her name when they came in the door

Teddy worked the warehouses over on Route 9,
smoked his pipe at night, watched the PBS

and in the cosmos the solar flares rippled
into dark andromedas as infinity expanded

Thursdays with the girls at the bingo halls
over in East Greenbush, Albany, Renssalaer

Sara, Sheri, and TJ (junior), one after the other,
little league in the summers, then drag races,
military bases and college, moving to distant cities
as storms rage the surface of Jupiter, bilious
explosions of vapor and light on Venus horizons,
phone calls on Sundays and Teddy in a plot
over in the bone yard right beneath a maple tree,
a little space beside him waiting

just for her

Jane Schermerhorn, never did mind the long
drives into Albany with the girls, country
music on the radio, a feeling of peace at the end
of the day, a few minutes where she could be
any Jane from any town, but going home
felt good too: familiar, safe, small, eternal

until it wasn't

long walks by the house where she grew up
every day, doctor's orders, keep the blood

moving and the mind working, visits from
Sheri and Sara now and then, daffodils in the yard,
a robot to vacuum and another in her hand,
the light of the TV keeping her company on
the long nights alone—too alone by the end

found on a Monday, joined Terry on a Thursday
bingo nights long behind her anyway, so why not?
right beneath a maple: convenient, cute, small, eternal

saltbox for sale, John Street: open house on Sunday

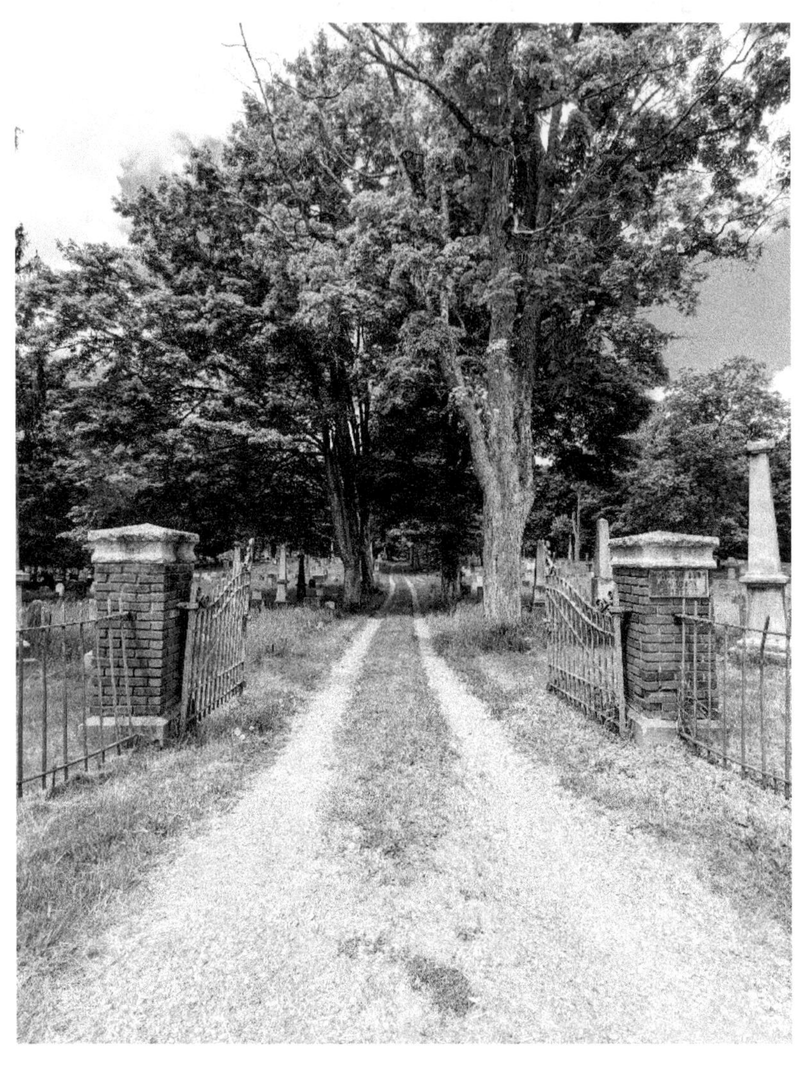

’85 Honda

maybe it’s the oxidized scent of rust
choking off the August air wafting
through the open bay door, but down
here underneath another blue Honda
hatchback there are little floating
stars in my eyes, a grayscale vignette
around the edges of existence where
the days don’t go by like they used to,
faster and faster—no, down here they
compress, close in, choke off the light
real slow, a giant boa constrictor with
infinite patience until there’s no air,
no time, no sky left, just a world of
bent mufflers, soot and salt, scorched oil,
grease burrowed into knuckles and cuts
you can only find through the layers of
grime with a heavy spray of carb cleaner
—you’ll know right where they are then,
trust me—and maybe this is all there is,
a parade of wrenches busting knuckles
for pennies on the dollar, angry phone
calls about late parts, dire needs, bills
unpaid as the Honda rolls out the door
and another rolls in, the breeze through
the bay window warm and promising,
just not promising anything to me here
in this garage where time races forward,
stops dead, but never goes back to the
cool springtime by the river when you
were young and I was young and we
almost made it out of this town, almost,
almost closing time, almost dinner time,
almost time to go to sleep so we can do
this again, crawl under the dark belly of an
‘85 Honda hatchback to pry away the guts
of failure, patch it together, get it back on
the road, a few more miles to get it right

Blood of Nostalgia

round we walked in concentric displays of costumes, gathered in the American Legion on the night before Halloween, decorations decades old hanging above, vibrant palimpsest of celebrations, hallucinations of ages past and gone, the bones of the men who first hung them lying pale in the graveyard at the edge of town, and round we go in our youthful parade until the music stops and the candy flows, gushing from pinatas, heaved into bowls, prizes awarded: prettiest, scariest, silliest, and best, music mashing and apples bobbling until our mothers led us into the night, straight home to bed because it wasn't Halloween yet, not *yet*, all the beating hearts under floorboards and in our chests would have to wait another day, another night, the moon slipping through the grip of the distant treeline at Nassau's edge one more time before we'd take the streets and hold tight, savor the night air, drink it like vampires, the blood of nostalgia, giving us the speed it takes to evade the grave and fill our pillowcases with sugar hope and happiness until one day we'll wake up and it's too late, it's all gone, and round we walk in concentric displays of another kind, shrouded by dreams and moonlight until we also fade to darkness in the great parade of time

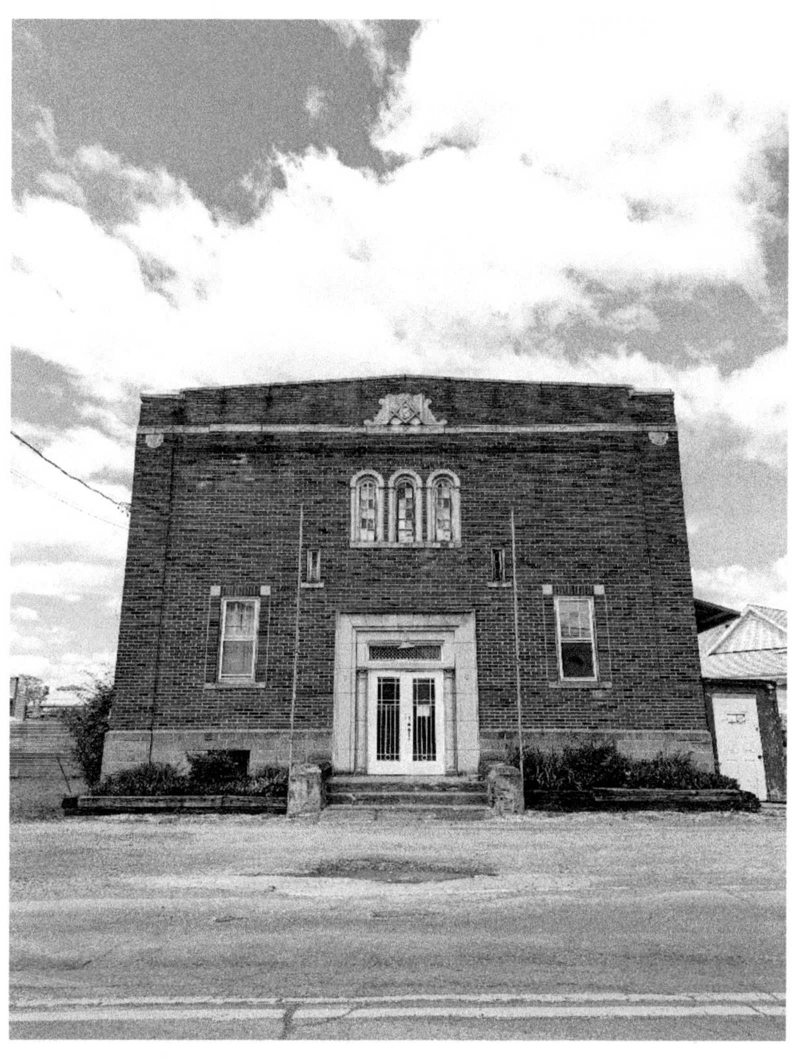

The Front Window

don't look out that front window
it only shows the yard, the two
old barrels full of dirt and flowers
that haven't bloomed in six years

don't look out that window at the
parking lot behind St. Mary's, the shadows
looming there from Sundays past
and the nightmares you prayed away

don't look beyond those curtains
where Freddie McHale's T-bird used
to rumble waiting for you, a ring
in his pocket, silver lost and gone

don't look beyond the wallpaper of
this room, your childhood bed, then
your grandmother's before she died,
and now yours again, yellow and silent

don't look out that front window at
Phillip's Street, the places it could lead
but won't, the hopes it once offered but
no longer can, the streetlight flicking on

don't look out there, you whisper in the night
you had a chance to make it right and now
the walls hum with age as you close your eyes
and dream of a Nassau that no longer exists

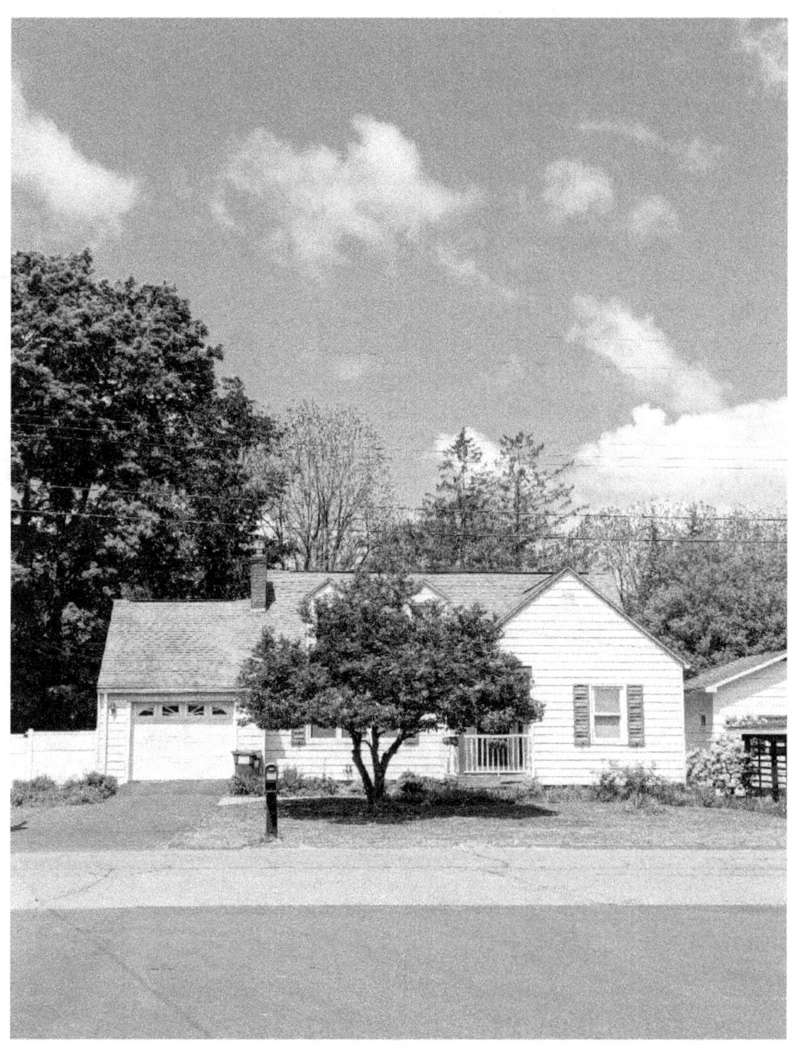

Witch House

that's what our sisters called it
late that one night when we all
wandered through town, parents
occupied by backyards and beer,
dusk stretching for days while we
spied the beautiful old home, the
witch house, fading yet immaculate
with fine woodwork and colorful
paint, and we never did see who
lived there, not a witch most likely
but a mysterious neighbor hiding
from the village concerns, holding
on to some past life that we darting
children would never understand
until we too lost too much, strayed
too far, and ached for all those lost
backyard nights of laughter and beer
and fireflies that blinked and ate the
hours, minutes, seconds of our youth

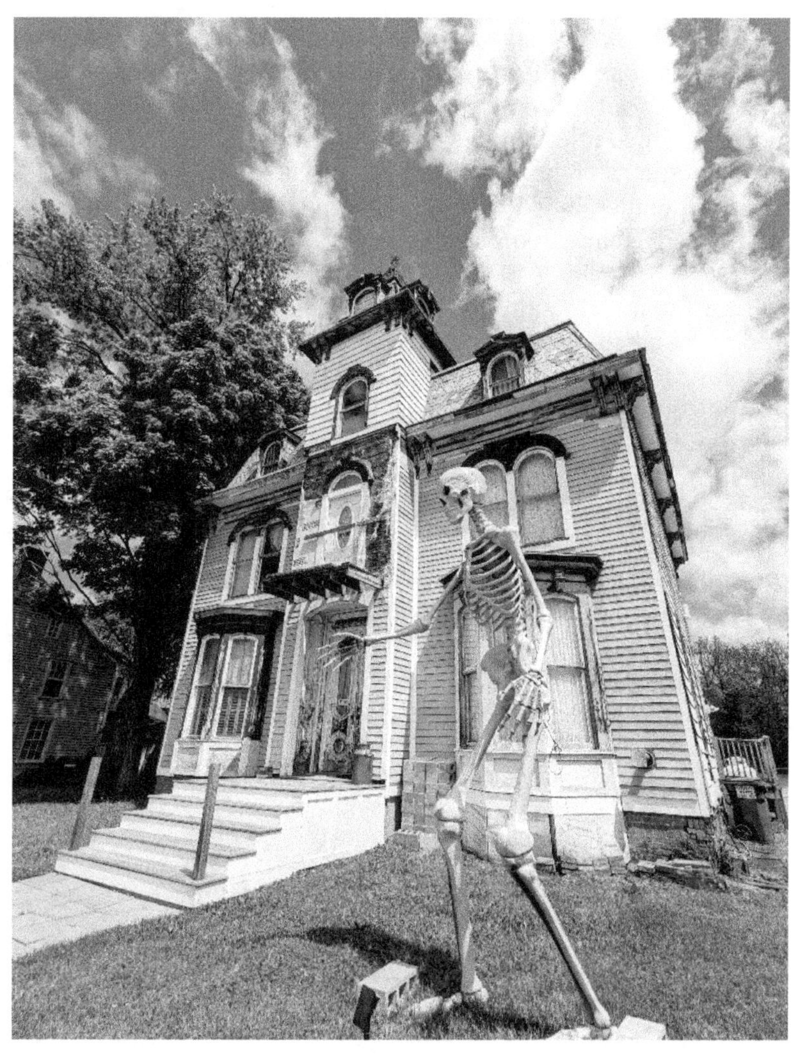

Concession

seas of dandelions heavy in summer's light glinting from metal dugout rooftops, half-crowds cheering from the wooden stands and another infield pop fly is caught, the rush back into the dugouts while I idle a moment longer, lost in daydreams of pirates and rolling seas of the Caribbean off the isle of Tortuga, shrinking away from taller, louder boys shoving me toward the bench, angry at my indifference, too close to the championship for screwups, too close to making the traveling team, the school team, the college team, their entire lives traced back to the summer of 1989 in Nassau when one pop fly missed in right field could make or break a life—but not my life, asking to sit out the next inning, blaming anything, my stomach, why not, and watching the others bat one after another from behind wire fencing as I edge my way quietly to the concession stand for the only thing that actually matters on small town Saturdays in June: a cherry red slush puppy and a spot of shade behind the cinderblock hut, the single maple tree there and a black and brown fuzzy caterpillar working its way up the trunk into the green oblivion above as somewhere a crowd cheers, someone has won, but I'm too busy sucking the dregs of cherry ice through the straw, content to turn away from glory to find something else entirely

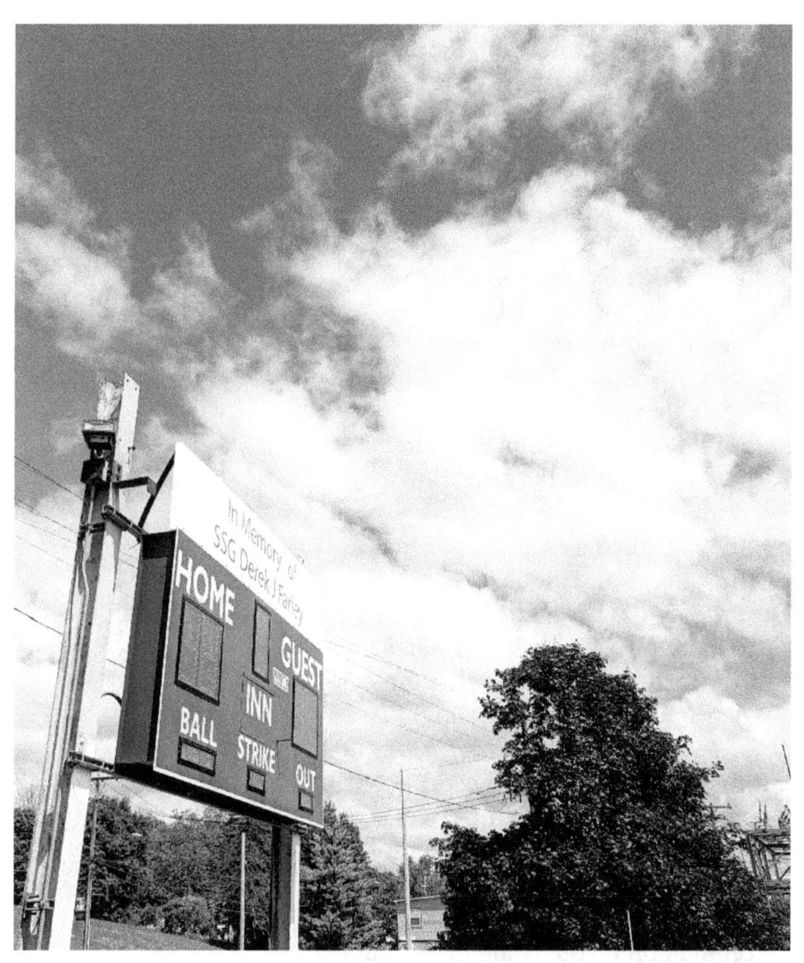
In Memory of
SSG Derek J Farley
HOME
GUEST
INN
BALL
STRIKE
OUT

Nightmares on Elm Street

wasn't long after
    the fourth of July
when they robbed the bank
    at the end of Elm Street
just four doors down

I was asleep at the time
    back when I'd nap right there
on the couch dad pushed
    onto the front porch after
mom moved away for six months
    while they "figured things out"
but all I heard were squealing tires
    then nothing 'til the sirens

but they'd killed a man inside
    the bank, some guy back from
Desert Storm who made a bad move
    to stop the robbers and failed,
so they shot him twice, a teller too,
    and then took off for the highway

but they caught them because
    Jessica and Karla up the street saw
their license plate, make and model,
    and they were the big celebrities in
town while I just felt dumb for sleeping
    on the porch couch and dreaming
of being late for school, like a fool

they had a wake for the guy
    who got shot in the funeral home
three door down from us
    right across from where he died
and I was just telling Karla how
    creepy that was—like what if he came
back as a zombie, angry at the world—

when we all heard the
news that the killers had escaped,
two of them at least, the third dying
while climbing a barbed-wire fence

the whole town ran home, terrified
that the killers would come
back to Nassau for revenge on those kids
who spotted their plates and
turned them in to the cops

every kid in town went into hiding
that night, afraid they'd be mistaken
for the rats (no longer the heroes)
and so I sat in my bedroom overlooking
Elm Street listening to my dad
yell with our mom on the phone
about when she'd be back, about how all
us kids missed her, needed her, but
in truth he just needed help keeping
the house afloat on his own, and we
loved our mom but it was kinda nice having
a summer to roam mostly unwatched,
and I almost picked up the phone upstairs to
say so and tell our mom to enjoy her
vacation (it was no vacation) when the streetlights
outside all came on at once, a magical
moment, the sun setting, the shadows growing
long, and a car I didn't know slowed to
a stop in the middle of Elm Street,
the silhouettes of two men inside

I panicked, pulling the curtains
closed as my dad's muffled argument
continued, and I watched the car,
waited as it idled, sprinklers next door
hissing in the thick summer air
and the call downstairs ended when
my dad slammed the phone

into the cradle, swearing, muttering,
and pacing through the house

then silence
until the car
slowly moved further
up the street

my bedroom light came on
just then and I screamed and
turned to see my dad there
annoyed and telling me there was
pizza on the way from Village
Pizza II, and to keep an eye out for
the delivery driver and
tell the others when it was here,
that he'd be in the basement
fixing his old ice fishing tip-ups

but even as the bell rang
when the pizza guy arrived, I sat
in my darkened room unable
to move, pizza being no motivation
for facing all else that waited for us
beyond that door, those streetlights,
the bank and funeral home at
the end of Elm Street, and the big wide
world beyond Nassau town

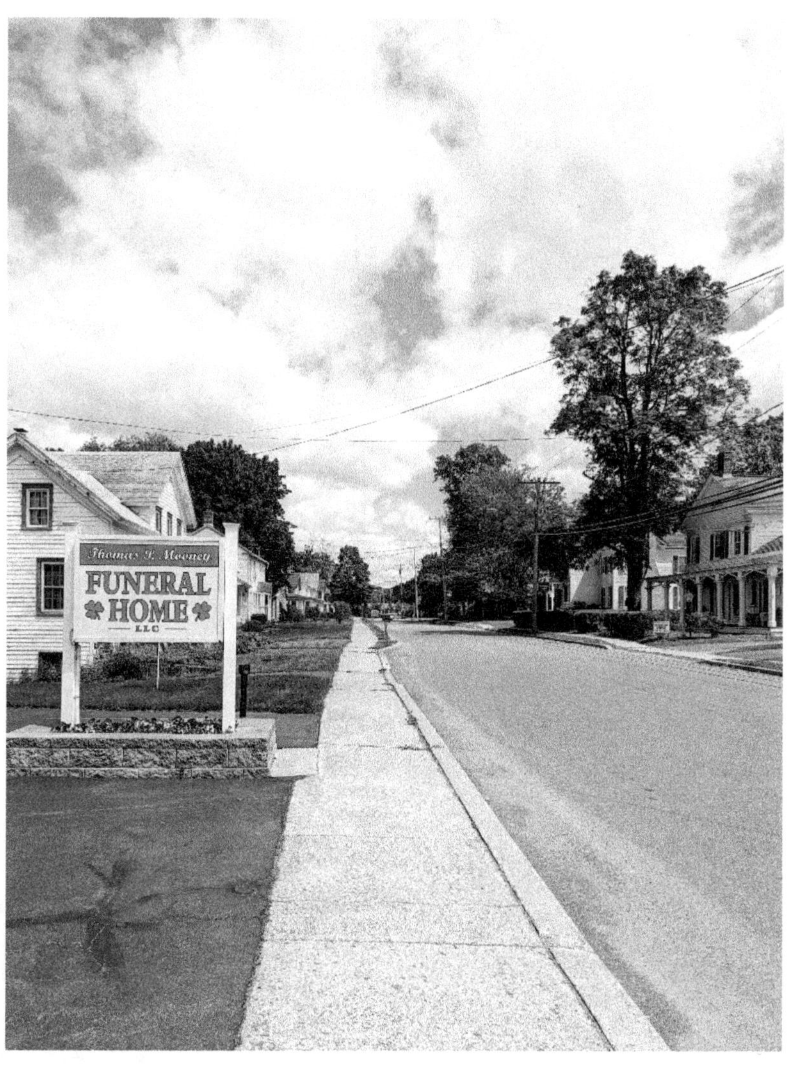
FUNERAL
HOME
LLC

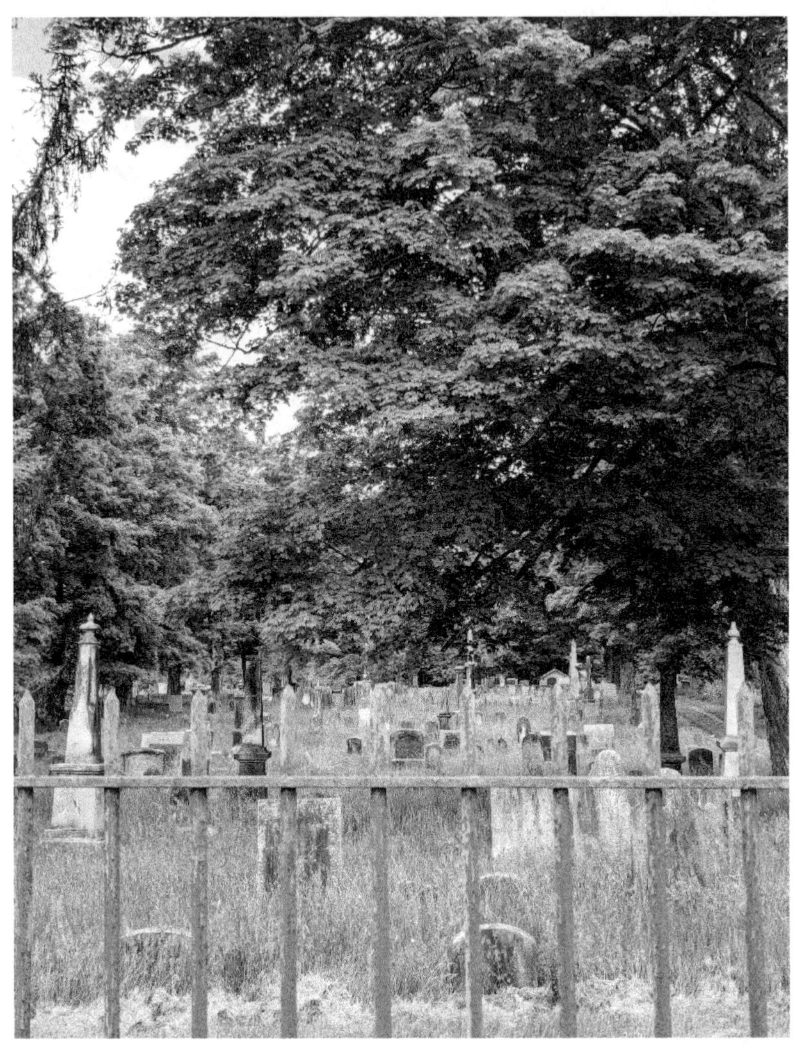

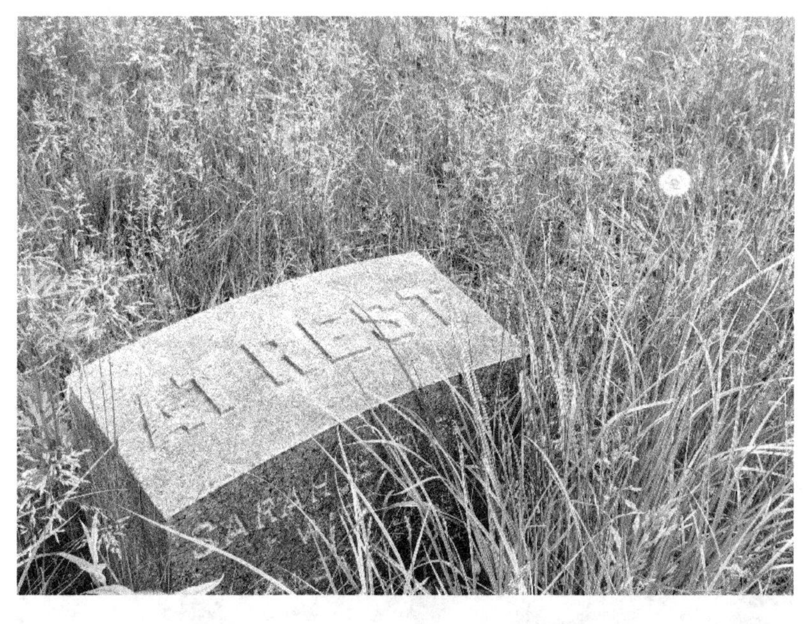
AT REST

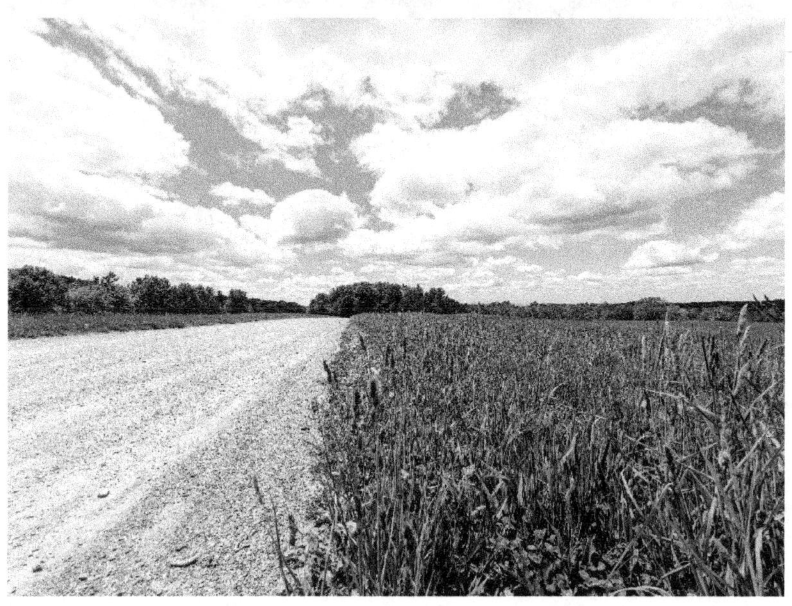

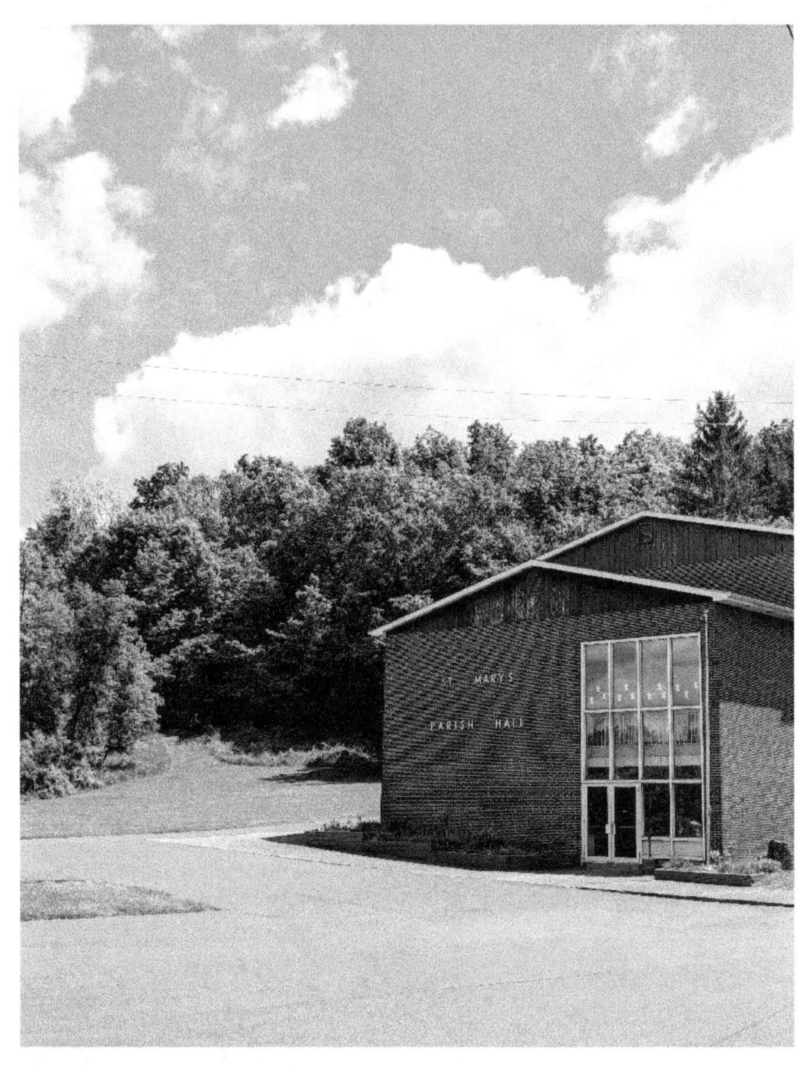
ST MARY'S
PARISH HALL

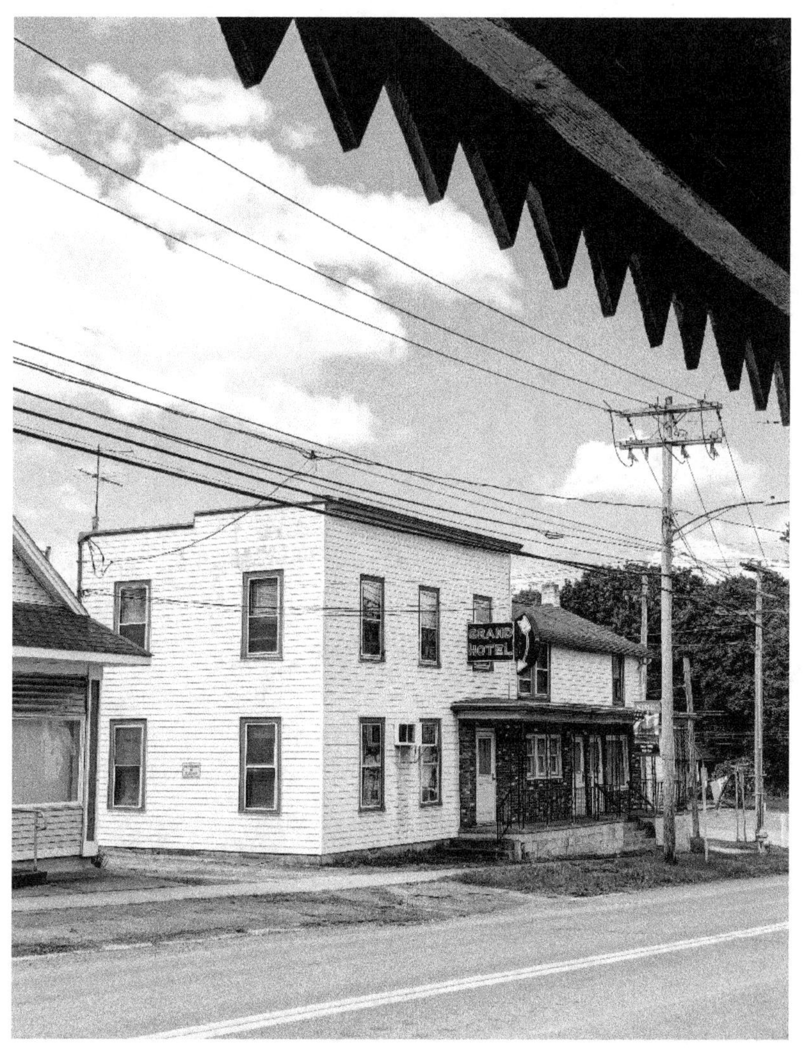
GRAND
HOTEL

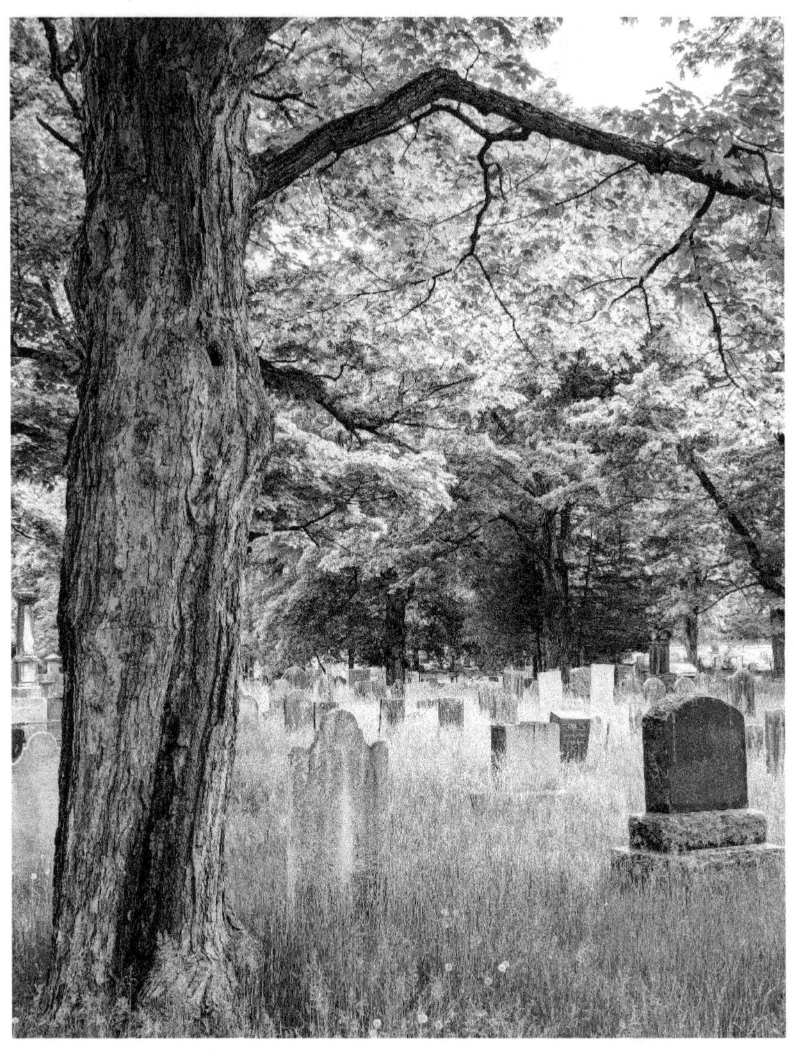

James H Duncan is the editor of *Hobo Camp Review*, a former editor with *Writer's Digest*, and the author of *Cistern Latitudes, Proper Etiquette in the Slaughterhouse Line, Vacancy, Both Ways Home, Beyond the Wounded Horizon,* and *We Are All Terminal But This Exit Is Mine*, among other books of fiction and poetry. He currently resides in upstate New York where he writes novels and reviews indie bookstores for his blog, The Bookshop Hunter. For more, visit www.jameshduncan.com.

"The Furnace of Your Heart" and "Village Video" appeared in *San Pedro River Review*
"Bailey's Hardware" appeared in *Nixes Mate Review*
"Hand Me Downs" appeared in *Chiron Review*
"Johnny '89" appeared in *Night Owl Narrative*
"Cherry Dip" appeared in *Misfit Magazine*
"Concession" appeared in *Book of Matches*

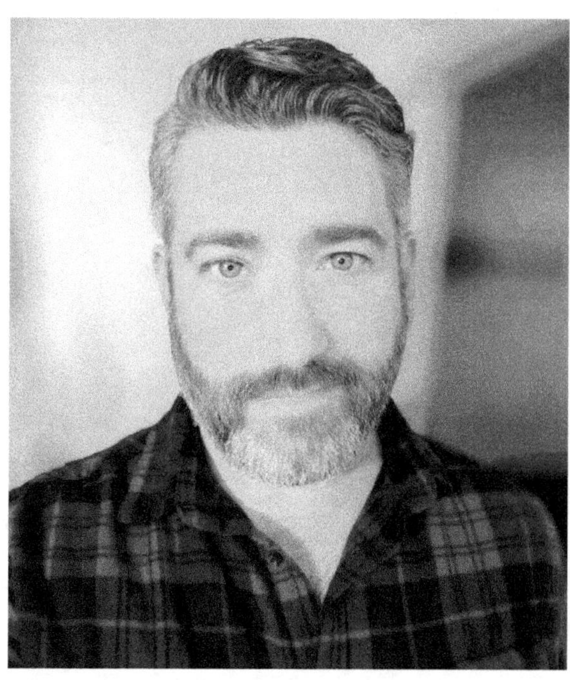

www.ingramcontent.com/pod-product-compliance
Lightning Source LLC
LaVergne TN
LVHW050610100826
845148LV00015B/3202

* 9 7 9 8 2 1 8 4 5 5 6 5 1 *